Revival
and
Missions

LIVING HISTORY THREADS

Revival and Missions

ISBN 978-1-935972-06-8

Author: Esther Bean

Credits: © The Trustees of the British Museum: 1, 3b, 10; Bunyan Ministries: 2, 3t; Princeton University Library: 5b; © New Room/John Wesley's Chapel, Bristol, UK: 7; Courtesy of Bridwell Library Special Collections, Perkins School of Theology, Southern Methodist University: 8; © British Library Board. All Rights Reserved: 9; Courtesy of American Tract Society Archives, Texas Baptists Historical Collection: 11t; Rare Books and Special Collections Division of the Library of Congress, Washington, DC: 11b; The John Newton Project www.johnnewton.org: 12; Courtesy of the Moody Bible Institute Crowell Library Archives: 16l, 16r, 17b; Courtesy of the George R. Brunk II Collection: 18, 19t, 19c, 19b; Archives of the Billy Graham Center, Wheaton, Illinois: 23, 35b; The Moravian Archives, Bethlehem: 24; Southern Baptist Historical Library and Archives, Nashville, Tennessee: 29t; The George Müller Charitable Trust: 31t; © Trustees of the National Library of Scotland: 33; Dohnavur Fellowship: 36; Wikimedia Commons/Creative Commons/San Jose (ed. by Kyle Brubaker): All Maps

Cover design: Kyle Brubaker
Cover picture: John Sartain, *Zeisberger preaching to the Indians*. Engraving.

Living History Threads is a history curriculum developed by Faith Builders Resource Group. For more information about the *Living History Threads*, email livinghistory@fbep.org or phone 877-222-4769.

Distributed by:
Christian Learning Resource
28500 Guys Mills Road
Guys Mills, PA 16327
www.christianlearning.org
877-222-4769

Copyright © 2011 by Faith Builders Resource Group.

Revival
and
Missions

Name: Tina Marei Miller

School: Riverview Christian School

Grade: 4th Grade

George Whitefield preaching

Revival

John Bunyan

1628 – 1688

John Bunyan was an outspoken preacher who was put in prison because the church authorities did not like his preaching. During his 12 years in prison, he wrote his best-known book, *Pilgrim's Progress*. It has been translated into more languages than any other book, except the Bible. He wrote close to 60 other books about the Christian life as well.

LIVED IN
England

John Bunyan in prison

Pilgrim arriving at the Wicket Gate

John Bunyan's cottage

Jonathan Edwards

1703 – 1758

Jonathan Edwards was a preacher, theologian, and missionary to American Indians. Attending one of his services would have given you lots to watch and think about. People in the audience often fainted or swooned while Edwards was preaching. There was much discussion about whether these unusual happenings were good or not. Jonathan Edward's most famous sermon was entitled "Sinners in the Hands of an Angry God".

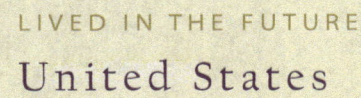

LIVED IN THE FUTURE
United States

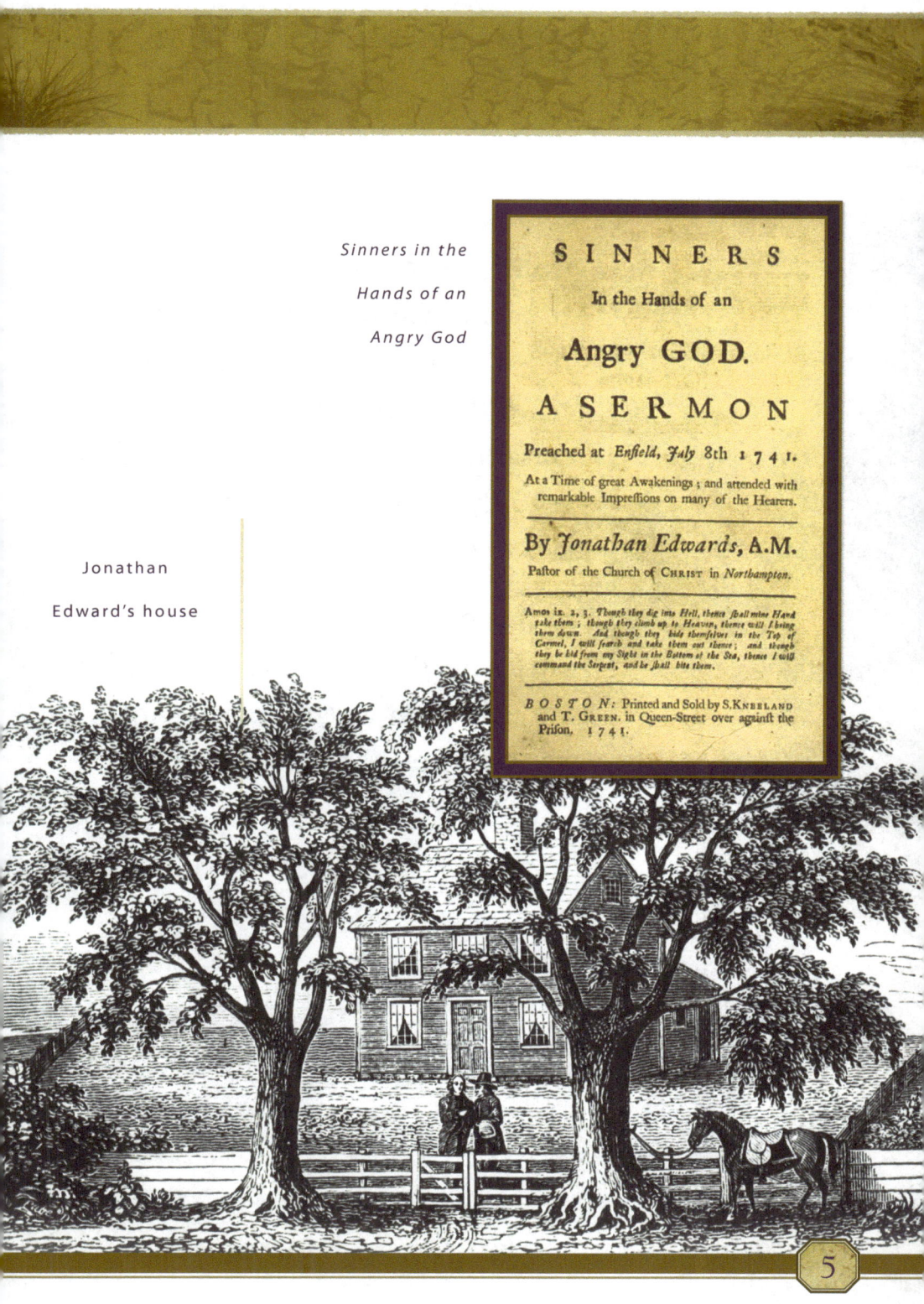

Sinners in the Hands of an Angry God

Jonathan Edward's house

John Wesley

1703 – 1791

John Wesley was rescued from a fire when he was five years old. He often said he was a "brand plucked from the burning". His mother, Susanna Wesley, is remembered as a godly woman who took time for her children.

John Wesley's beliefs were influenced by the Moravians, but he is known as the founder of the Methodists.

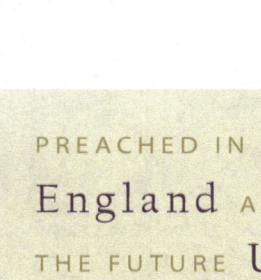

PREACHED IN
England AND
THE FUTURE United States

John Wesley preached for a short time in Georgia in the future United States, but was not successful. He returned to England where he continued his preaching. Wesley is remembered for traveling by horse around England in order to preach the Gospel and for preaching outside. At first, the idea of outdoor preaching seemed strange. The gospel was supposed to be preached in a church! During his lifetime, John Wesley rode horseback over 250,000 miles and preached close to 40,000 sermons.

Statue of John Wesley on horseback

Charles Wesley

1707 – 1788

Charles Wesley, a brother of John Wesley, was a preacher also. However, he is known more for his music than for his preaching. Charles Wesley wrote over 5,000 hymns. Many hymn books have some of his poetry.

LIVED IN
England

How many of these songs do you know?

- And Can it be that I Should Gain?
- Arise, My Soul, Arise
- A Charge to Keep I Have
- Christ, the Lord, is Risen Today
- Come, Thou Almighty King
- Come, Thou Long Expected Jesus
- Gentle Jesus, Meek and Mild
- Hark! The Herald Angels Sing
- Jesus, from Whom all Blessings Flow
- Jesus, Lover of my Soul
- Love Divine, All Loves Excelling
- O For a Thousand Tongues
- Rejoice, the Lord is King!

The Sky was Purpled O'er -excerpt from Charles Wesley's works

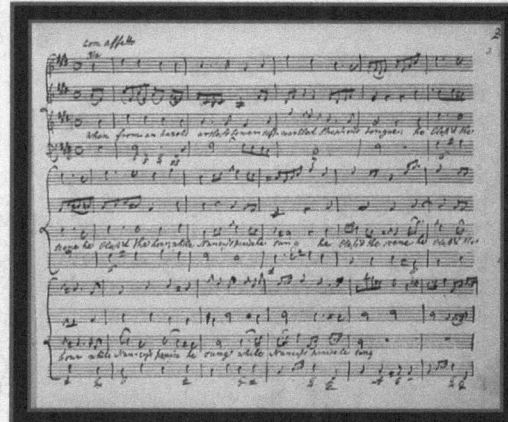

George Whitefield

1714 – 1770

George Whitefield was very instrumental in the beginning of the Great Awakening in the future United States. The Great Awakening was a time of great religious revival.

George Whitefield wasn't always allowed to preach in church, so he preached outdoors, sometimes to crowds of 20,000-30,000 people.

BORN IN
England

PREACHED IN THE FUTURE
United States

Sometimes, when he preached, people threw rotten eggs, stones, and even pieces of dead cat at him. The picture to the right shows a collapsible pulpit that he used. It's estimated that George Whitefield preached 2,000 sermons from that pulpit. Many people were influenced by his teaching.

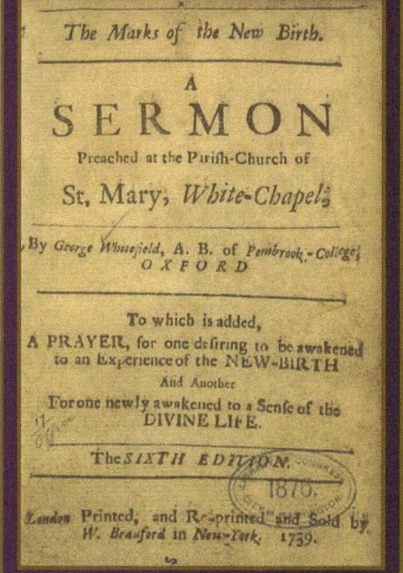

A sermon by George Whitefield

John Newton

1725 – 1807

John Newton was the captain of a slave ship. He transported Africans to places where they would be sold into slavery.

On one voyage, there was a terrible storm that motivated him to cry out to God for deliverance. After God answered his prayer, Newton began to read the Bible. He broke some of his bad habits, but he didn't stop his involvement in the slave business. God kept working in his heart and John Newton made other commitments to Him in the years following.

LIVED IN

England

Later in his life, John Newton looked back with regret at the slave transporting business. He wrote a confession describing the horrible conditions of the slaves on the ships.

Newton's song, "Amazing Grace," is a testimony of how God, in His love and grace, took Newton as a sinner and rescued him from sin. Christians today sing "Amazing Grace" as a reminder of all God has done in His great love for all people.

The slave deck of the ship *Wildfire*

Fanny Crosby

1820 – 1915

Fanny Crosby had a remarkable ability to memorize and to write poetry. She was blinded as a baby because of an eye infection and harmful treatment. Fanny's grandmother vividly described the world around Fanny, read the Bible to her, and helped her to memorize.

Fanny Crosby memorized five chapters of the Bible every week. When she was an adult, she knew by memory Genesis, Exodus,

LIVED IN THE
United States

Fanny Crosby
in her study

"Oh what a happy soul I am,
Although I cannot see;
I am resolved that in this world
Contented I will be.
How many blessings I enjoy,
That other people don't;
To weep and sigh because I'm blind,
I cannot, and I won't."

Fanny Crosby (8 yrs old)

Leviticus, Numbers, Deuteronomy, Proverbs, Matthew, Mark, Luke, and John, as well as many other passages.

When you write a story or poem, you probably write it on paper and then change it. Fanny did all of this in her head. She sometimes had 12 poems that she was working on mentally before she would recite them to be recorded. At the time of her death, Fanny Crosby had written over 8,000 poems. It's hard to know the exact amount because she used possibly over 100 pseudonyms since people making hymn books didn't like to use so many songs from one person.

Dwight L. Moody

1837 – 1899

D. L. Moody began his work for the Lord when he became a Sunday school teacher. He invited and collected boys from the streets of Chicago to be his class. Within a year, he had 650 people in the Sunday school and 60 helpers.

Sunday School class

He preached to large audiences in Great Britain and in the United States. He worked as a team with Ira Sankey; D. L. Moody preached

LIVED IN THE
United States

and Ira Sankey led the singing. Stadiums of 10,000-20,000 people filled to hear D. L. Moody speak. He met Charles Spurgeon and Hudson Taylor. He supported the China Inland Mission and encouraged his congregation to volunteer to be missionaries.

D. L. Moody founded Moody Bible Institute. It is a Bible college and also does book publishing and radio broadcasting.

All photos courtesy of the Moody Bible Institute Crowell Library Archives.

Brunk Brothers

George R. Brunk II and Lawrence Brunk

George R. Brunk II
1912 – 2002

George R. Brunk II and his brother, Lawrence, held tent crusades from 1951-1981. In those 30 years, they held more than 100 crusades across North America. A crusade in a community lasted several weeks, and often people would attend most of the nights. Before he died, he was the editor of a magazine called *The Sword and Trumpet*. Perhaps George R. Brunk II preached in your community.

LIVED IN THE
United States

The largest tent could seat 6,000 people

This campaign was held for weeks. On the last night over 2,220 cars crowded into the parking area.

In Ohio 6,000 people filled the tent most evenings

19

China Inland Missionaries

MISSIONS

David Zeisberger

1721 – 1808

David Zeisberger moved to Georgia when he was seventeen years old. He lived with his family, and soon after they moved, he helped to begin a Moravian settlement in Bethlehem, Pennsylvania.

For sixty-two years, he was a missionary to the American Indians. Since he lived among them, his descriptions of their lives are valuable for us today. When there were dangerous conflicts

BORN IN
Moravia
(now part of the Czech Republic)

MISSIONARY IN THE
United States

among the tribes or with the settlers, David helped the American Indians to relocate in Michigan and Ontario.

During the Revolutionary War, David Zeisberger was imprisoned by the British, and some of his converts were rounded up by the Patriots. When a hundred Christian Lenape returned to their homes to harvest crops, they were captured by the American militia. Ninety-six Christian Lenape were killed by the American troops while kneeling and praying.

David Zeisberger lived with the Mohawks, Iroquois, Algonquian, and Lenape (Delaware). He studied their languages, wrote dictionaries, and worked with translation.

Zeisberger preaching to the Indians

William Carey

1761 – 1834

William Carey is known as the "Father of modern missions". In India, he worked and preached for seven years before the first person became a Christian. Working with his first convert, Krishna Pal, William Carey translated the Bible into Bengali. One time, a fire destroyed their printing presses and years of their work. But William Carey did not give up.

BORN IN
England

MISSIONARY TO
India

John's Gospel in Sanskrit

He printed the Bible in Sanskrit and other languages. He also translated Indian writings into English. William Carey founded Serampore College which trained Indian pastors and educated people regardless of their caste. He worked to stop infant sacrifice and *suttee*. *Suttee* was the Indians' word for burning a woman alive on her husband's funeral pyre.

> Expect great things from God; attempt great things for God.
>
> *William Carey*

Serampore College

Adoniram Judson

1788 – 1850

Adoniram Judson was a missionary in Burma (now Myanmar) for almost 40 years. He and Ann were the first American Protestant missionaries to travel overseas. His life inspired many Americans to support missionaries or to become foreign missionaries themselves. Adoniram knew Latin, Greek, and Hebrew, and studied the Burmese language for 12 hours a day for 3 years in preparation to preach and translate the Bible.

BORN IN THE
United States

MISSIONARY IN
Burma
(now Myanmar)

When Burma and England were at war, Adoniram Judson was imprisoned for a year and a half. During this time, his wife died. She had been able to speak fluently and was friends with many Burmese ladies.

It was against the law for the Burmese people to change religions, so the church grew slowly. After the war, the church grew in the tribal areas rather than the Buddhist areas. After 24 years of hard work, the Burmese translation of the Bible was complete.

Ann Judson

John's Gospel

in Burmese

George Müller

1805 – 1898

George Müller is known for his strong faith in God. He believed that if he needed something, he should not tell anyone except God about the need. He relied on prayer alone to supply money for the children he cared for. There are many stories of how God miraculously answered his prayers. Many times, George received food only hours before the children were to be fed.

George Müller built orphanages for orphans in England. At one of the orphan centers, Ashley Down,

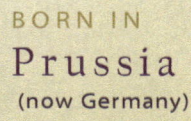

BORN IN
Prussia
(now Germany)

MISSIONARY IN
England

28

Orphans at Ashley Down

he and workers cared for 2,000 orphans. Altogether, he provided for 10,024 orphans.

When he was 70 years old, George Müller began 17 years of missionary travel to the United States, China, India, Japan, and Australia. He also gave much money to educate thousands of children. He supported 150 missionaries and supplied money for 64,000 Bibles, 85,000 Testaments, and 29 million religious books.

George Müller died penniless, but during his life he had received over £1.5 million (today worth about 150 million dollars) to help care for the orphans.

Five orphanages at Ashley Down

David Livingstone

1813 – 1873

David Livingstone studied hard and became a doctor before going to Africa as a missionary. He explored much of central Africa, making maps and noting scientific discoveries in his journal. He traveled into areas that had never before been explored.

At this time, Africans were being kidnapped from their homes and sold into slavery. One of David Livingstone's motivations

BORN IN
Scotland

MISSIONARY AND EXPLORER IN CENTRAL
Africa

in exploring central Africa was to help to end the slave trade. He said that stopping the slave trade would be better than any discovery.

He died in Zambia while searching for the source of the Nile River. His loyal attendants buried his heart in Africa, then carried his body 1,000 miles where it could be taken back for burial in England.

David Livingstone's map, made around 1863, of Lake Malawi

J. Hudson Taylor

1832 – 1905

J. Hudson Taylor dedicated his life to God and to China. He wrote to his sister, "If I had a thousand pounds, China should have it. If I had a thousand lives, China should have them. No! Not China, but Christ. Can we do too much for Him? Can we do enough for such a precious Saviour?" Hudson Taylor spent 51 years in China.

Before moving to China, Hudson Taylor prepared by studying medicine and living with little money. In China, he tried to be

BORN IN
England

MISSIONARY TO
China

sensitive to Chinese culture. He adopted their language and food and did not think that a new Christian must become like the Europeans. He dressed in Chinese clothes, which was rare for a missionary. He preached and treated people medically. He translated the New Testament into the Ningpo dialect, a language that is no longer spoken.

John's Gospel in Chinese

He founded the China Inland Mission. Like George Müller, he refused to ask for money, but depended only on God to supply his needs. All missionaries working with him needed to do the same. He influenced many English people to come to China. At the time of his death, there were 205 mission stations, over 800 missionaries, and 125,000 Chinese Christians.

Missionaries in Chinese clothes

Amy Carmichael

1867 – 1951

Amy Carmichael dedicated her life to God and to India's children. She received a letter from a young lady who thought she might want to become a missionary. The lady asked Amy, "What is missionary life like?" Amy replied, "Missionary life is simply a chance to die."

Amy Carmichael decided to go into mission work after hearing Hudson Taylor speak. She lived

BORN IN
Ireland

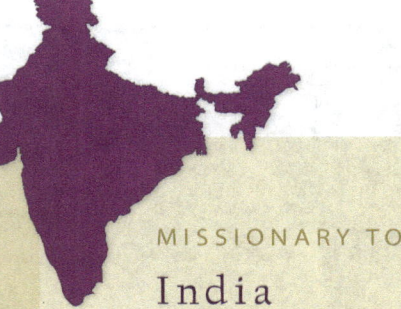

MISSIONARY TO
India

Indian Children

in India for 55 years with no furlough. She dressed in Indian clothes to be more easily accepted in Indian culture. As a child, she had prayed that God would change her brown eyes to blue, but later realized that it was to her advantage to have brown eyes.

She founded an orphanage, where she cared for over 1,000 children who were saved from dangerous situations. She founded a mission called Dohnavur Fellowship that continues today.

Amy Carmichael was always sickly, but 20 years before she died, she was injured in a fall. She was then confined to her bed and began to spend much of her time writing. Altogether, Amy wrote 35 books.

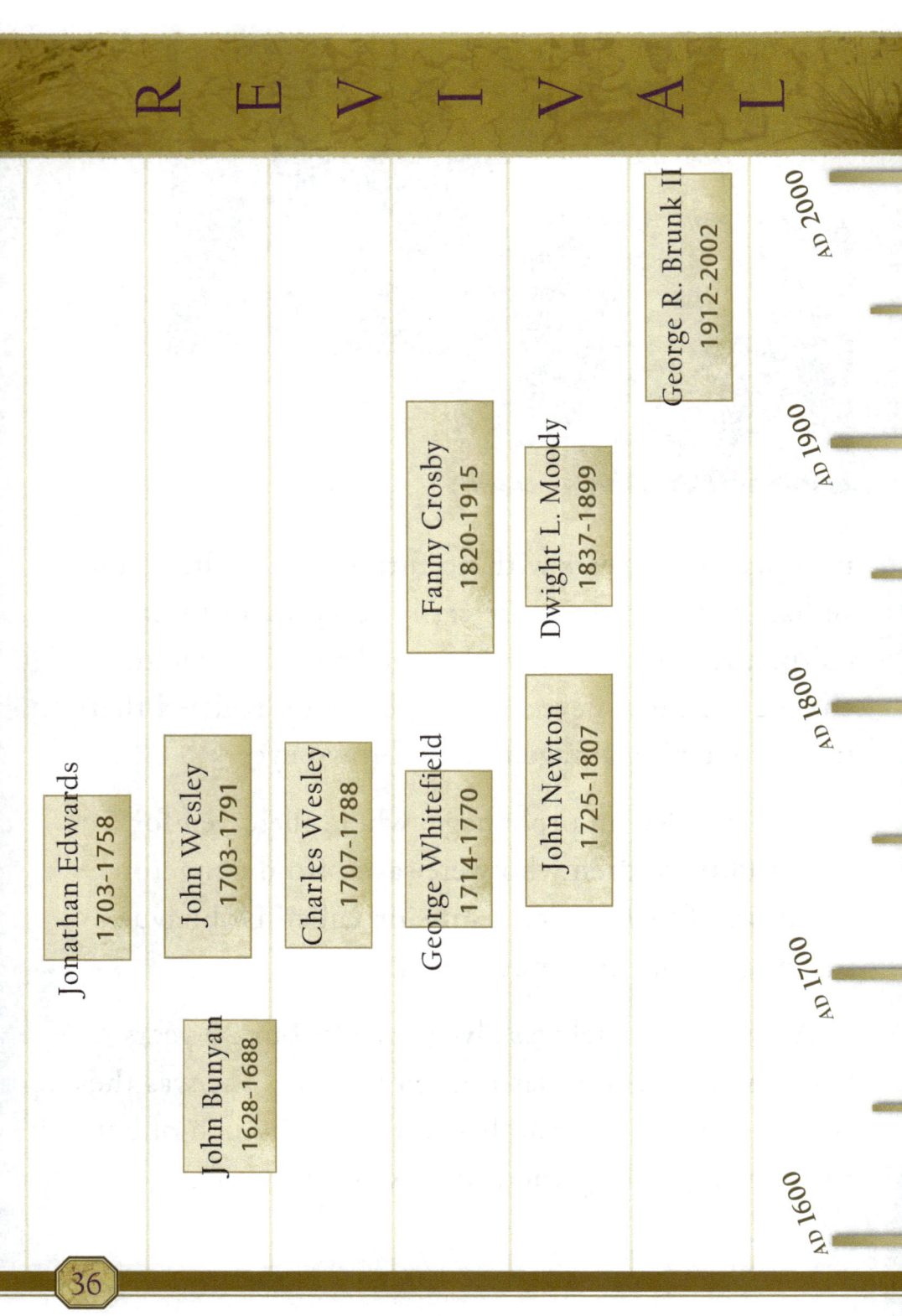

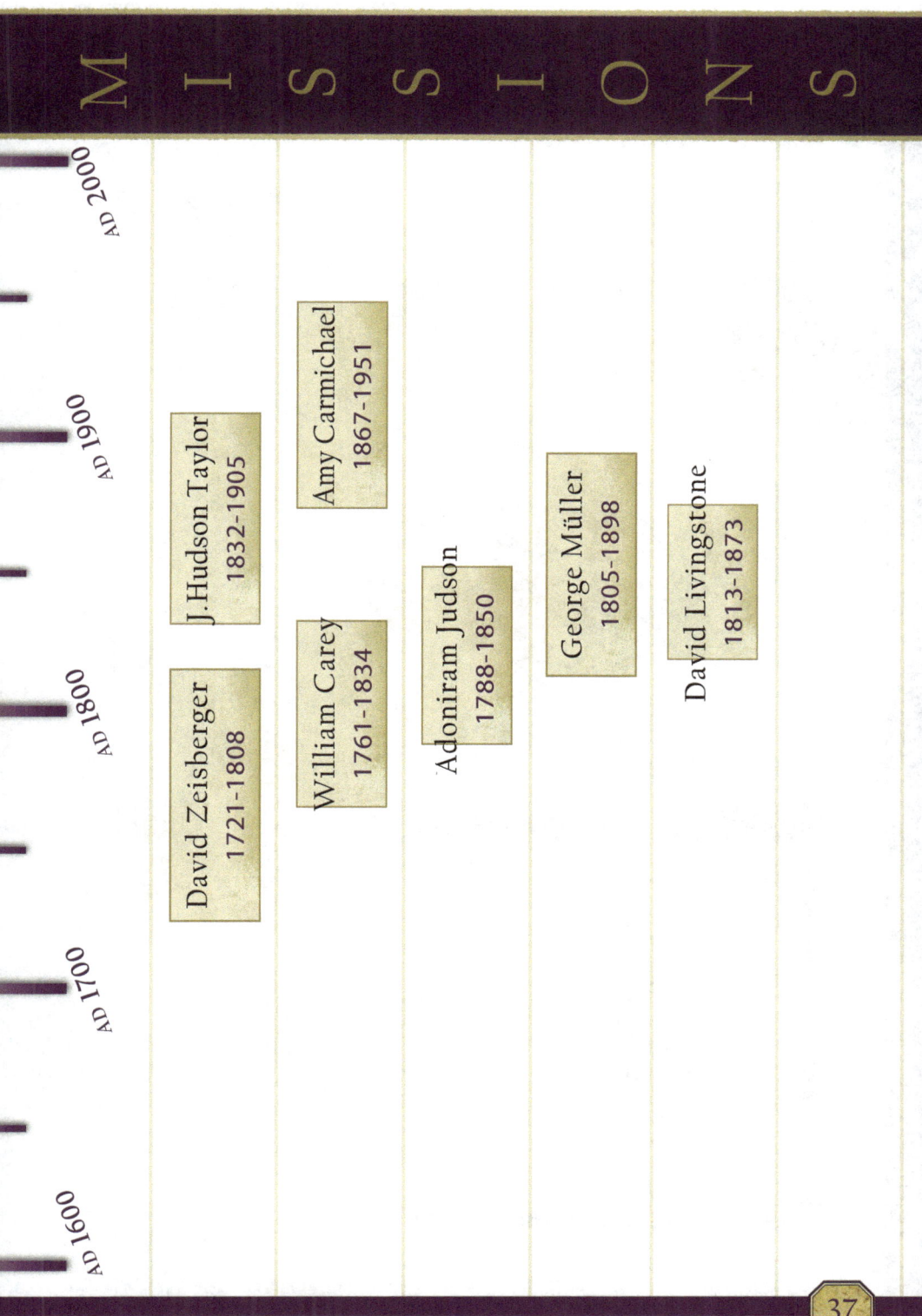

Missionary Travels

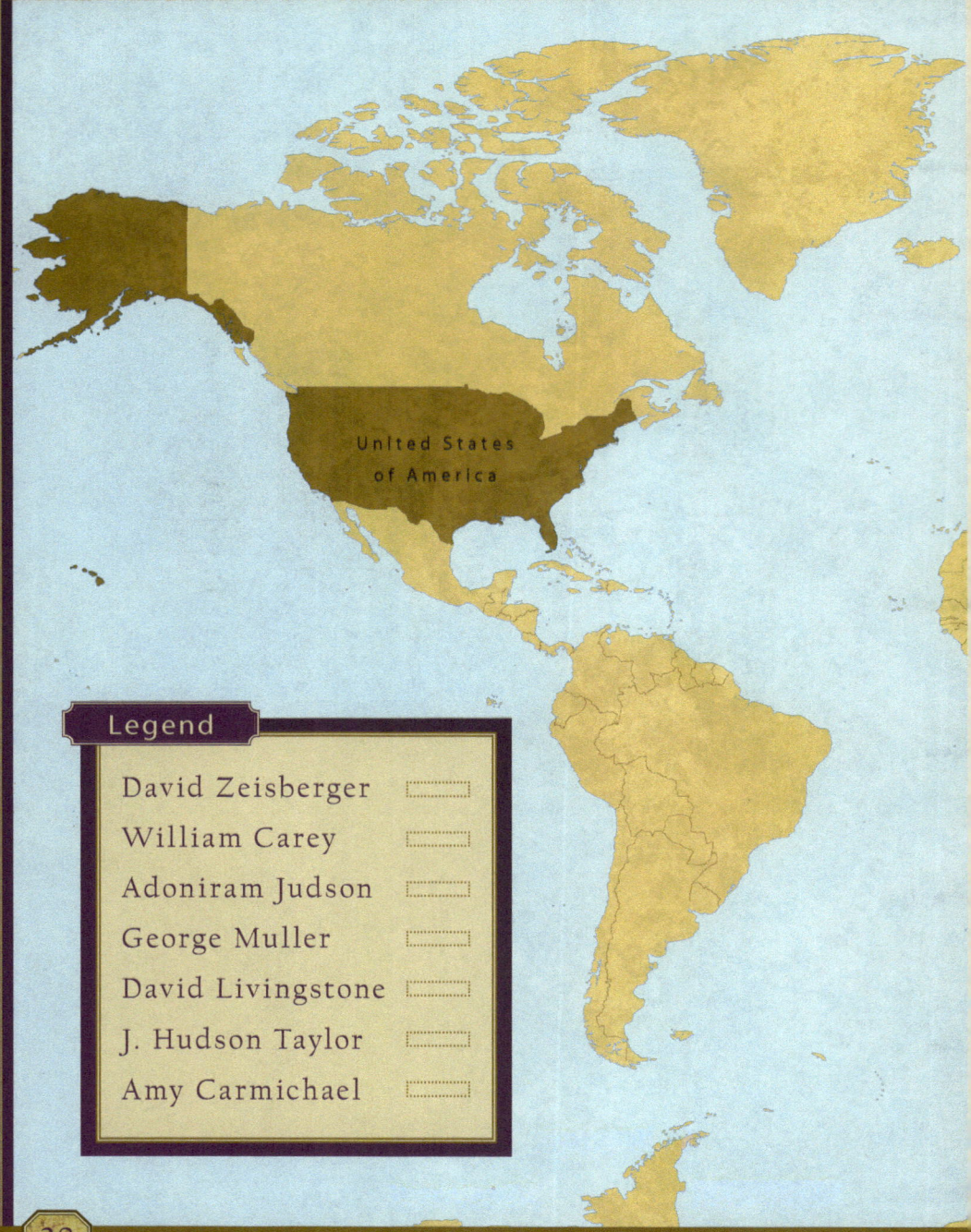

Ireland
Scotland
Germany
Czech Republic
England

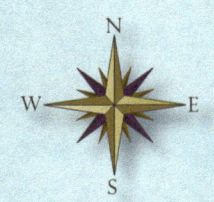

AFRICA

China
India
Myanmar